Space Circles

Learning About Radius and Diameter

Kerri O'Donnell

PowerMath™

The Rosen Publishing Group's
PowerKids Press™
New York

Published in 2004 by The Rosen Publishing Group, Inc.
29 East 21st Street, New York, NY 10010

Book Design: Ron A. Churley

Photo Credits: Cover, pp. 10, 27 (Neptune) © DigitalVision; p. 4 by Ron A. Churley; pp. 8, 12, 17 (both), 18, 20, 24, 29, 30 © PhotoDisc; pp. 8 (inset), 24 (inset) © Hulton/Archive; p. 12 (inset) © Wilson Goodwich/Index Stock; p. 15 (Moon) © H. Armstrong Roberts; p. 18 (inset) © Ron Russell/Index Stock; p. 21 © V.C.L./Taxi; p. 22 © NASA/Index Stock; pp. 27 (Triton), 28 © NASA/Roger Ressmeyer/Corbis.

Library of Congress Cataloging-in-Publication Data

O'Donnell, Kerri, 1972-
  Space circles : learning about radius and diameter / Kerri O'Donnell.
      p. cm. — (PowerMath)
Includes index.
Summary: Examines the relationship between diameter and radius by exploring and comparing the sizes of the planets and moons in the solar system.
  ISBN 0-8239-8985-2 (lib. bdg.)
  ISBN 0-8239-8878-3 (pbk.)
  6-pack ISBN: 0-8239-7387-5
  1. Diameter (Geometry)—Juvenile literature. 2. Radius
(Geometry)—Juvenile literature. 3. Solar system—Juvenile literature.
[1. Solar system. 2. Diameter (Geometry) 3. Radius (Geometry)] I.
Title. II. Series.
  QA484.O36 2004
  516—dc21

                                        200300268

Manufactured in the United States of America

Contents

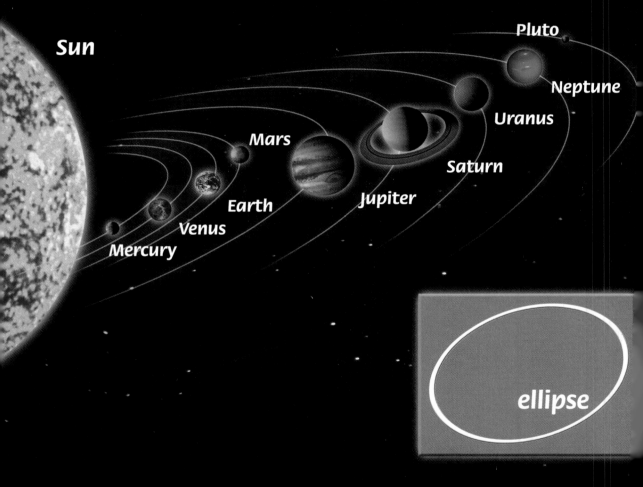

Sun

Mercury

Venus

Earth

Mars

Jupiter

Saturn

Uranus

Neptune

Pluto

ellipse

The paths of the planets as they orbit the Sun are
not shaped like circles. They are shaped like ovals, or
ellipses. This means that the planets move closer to and
farther away from the Sun as they orbit it.

Earth and Beyond

Earth is the planet on which we live. It is the fifth largest planet in our **solar system**, which is made up of our Sun, Earth, 8 other planets, many moons, and other small space objects. The Sun is the star at the center of our solar system. Earth and the other 8 planets travel around the Sun, each in its own orbit, or path. A planet called Mercury is closest to the Sun. Next is Venus, then Earth, Mars, Jupiter, Saturn, Uranus, Neptune, and finally Pluto.

We might think that Earth is huge, but compared to some of the other planets in the solar system, Earth is fairly small. We can use a measurement called **diameter** to help us compare the sizes of planets. Diameter is the distance of a straight line through the center of a round object. Since planets are round in shape, like circles, diameter is used to measure their size. In this book, we'll learn about the 9 planets in our solar system and their sizes by using diameter.

Diameter and Radius

Before we look at the planets, let's look at a circle to become more familiar with what diameter is. The diameter is the line that runs through the circle's center and has endpoints that lie on the outer edge of the circle. This is the widest part of the circle. The circle shown here has a diameter of 4 inches, which means that the line that goes through the center of the circle is 4 inches long.

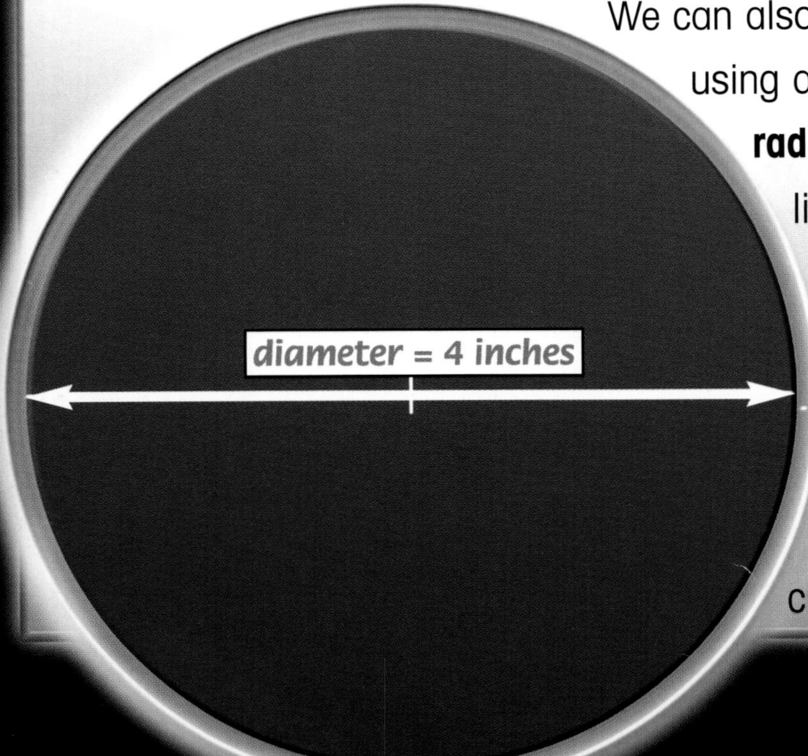

diameter = 4 inches

We can also measure the circle by using a distance called the **radius**. The radius is the line that extends from the center of the circle to a point on the outer edge of the circle. The radius is exactly $\frac{1}{2}$ the distance of the circle's diameter.

In this circle the radius is 2 inches, since it is $\frac{1}{2}$ of the circle's diameter of 4 inches. If you were to add the radius of a circle twice, you'd have the diameter: 2 inches + 2 inches = 4 inches (radius + radius = diameter). This is the same as multiplying the radius by 2. You can find the radius of a circle by dividing the diameter by 2. In this circle, dividing the diameter (4 inches) by 2 gives us a radius of 2 inches.

Now let's see how radius and diameter work by looking at the planets in our solar system.

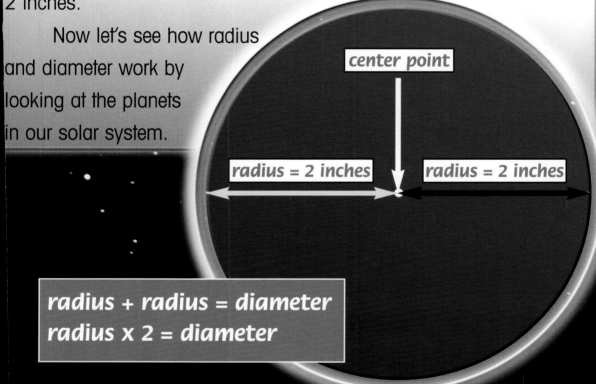

center point

radius = 2 inches

radius = 2 inches

radius + radius = diameter
radius x 2 = diameter

Mercury

Mercury is the fastest-moving planet in our solar system. Thousands of years ago, the Romans named the planet Mercury after the messenger of their gods, who was known for his quickness.

The Hottest Planets

The 4 planets that are closest to the Sun are Mercury, Venus, Earth, and Mars. These planets are made of rock and are relatively small compared to most of the other planets.

The planet closest to the Sun is Mercury. Mercury is very hot and dry. During the day, the temperature on Mercury can reach 800 degrees Fahrenheit, or 800°F. As Mercury orbits the Sun, its distance from the Sun ranges between 28,600,000 miles and 43,400,000 miles. It takes 88 Earth days for Mercury to orbit the Sun. That means that a year on Mercury is just 88 days long!

Mercury is the second smallest planet in the solar system. Only Pluto is smaller. Because Mercury is so small, it is often difficult for people on Earth to see the planet without a **telescope**. Scientists have discovered that Mercury measures about 3,030 miles across, which means its diameter is about 3,030 miles. Using this information, can you find the radius of Mercury? You can divide Mercury's diameter by 2 to get your answer.

$$
\begin{array}{r}
1{,}515 \\
2{\overline{)}\,3{,}030} \\
-2\phantom{{,}030} \\
\hline
1\,0 \\
-1\,0 \\
\hline
0\,3 \\
-2 \\
\hline
1\,0 \\
-1\,0 \\
\hline
0
\end{array}
$$

Mercury's radius is 1,515 miles.

The next closest planet to the Sun is Venus. It is also the closest planet to Earth. Like Mercury, Venus is made of rock. It shines more brightly in our night sky than any other planet or star and can be seen without a telescope. If a person looked at Venus through a telescope, they would be able to see the planet going through **phases** that make it look as if the planet's size and shape are changing. This is much like the phases our Moon goes through. What the Moon looks like depends on how much of its sunlit surface we can see from Earth.

Venus

While the paths of all the other planets in our solar system are shaped like ellipses, Venus's orbit around the Sun is almost circular. During its orbit, its distance from the Sun varies only a little, from 66,800,000 miles to 67,700,000 miles. It takes Venus about 225 Earth days to orbit the Sun once.

Venus is often called Earth's "twin" because both planets are about the same size. Scientist have discovered that Venus's radius is about 3,760 miles. We can find Venus's diameter in 2 ways—by using either addition or multiplication.

$$
\begin{array}{r}
3{,}760 \text{ miles (Venus's radius)} \\
+\ 3{,}760 \text{ miles (Venus's radius)} \\
\hline
7{,}520 \text{ miles (Venus's diameter)}
\end{array}
$$

$$
\begin{array}{r}
3{,}760 \text{ miles (Venus's radius)} \\
\times\quad 2 \\
\hline
7{,}520 \text{ miles (Venus's diameter)}
\end{array}
$$

Even though Mercury is the closest planet to the Sun, Venus is the hottest planet in the solar system. Its surface can be hotter than 864°F!

Planet Earth

Like Mercury and Venus, Earth is made of rock. Earth is about 93 million miles from the Sun and travels about 584 million miles in its orbit around the Sun. This orbit takes about 365 days, or 1 year. Although to us it feels as if Earth does not move at all, the planet is actually traveling over 66,000 miles an hour as it orbits the Sun. If you could drive a car that fast, you could get from New York City to Los Angeles in about $2\frac{1}{2}$ minutes!

Earth

As we learned on page 11, Earth is about the same size as Venus. In fact, Earth's diameter is only about 406 miles larger than Venus's diameter. Using the information on page 11, we can figure out how large Earth's diameter is by adding 406 miles to Venus's diameter of 7,520 miles.

$$\begin{array}{r} 7{,}520 \text{ miles} \\ +\ \ 406 \text{ miles} \\ \hline 7{,}926 \text{ miles} \end{array}$$

Earth's diameter is about 7,926 miles.

Can you find Earth's radius? Just divide Earth's diameter by 2.

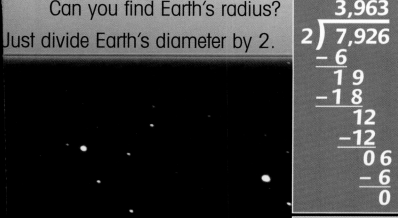

Earth's radius is 3,963 miles.

Although Venus and Earth are similar in size, Venus is much too hot to support plant or animal life as we know it. Earth's average temperature is about 59°F, which makes it

You've seen Earth's Moon in the night sky. The Moon orbits Earth in much the same way the 9 planets orbit the Sun. It moves at a speed of about 2,300 miles per hour! At that speed, it takes the Moon 27 days, 7 hours, and 43 minutes to complete 1 full orbit.

The Moon is held in its orbit by a force called **gravity**. Gravity is the force between 2 objects that attracts or pulls them toward each other. Earth's gravity is stronger than the Moon's gravity, which keeps the Moon in its orbit around Earth. Even though Earth's gravity is stronger than the Moon's, the Moon's gravity still affects Earth. The Moon's gravity causes the ocean's tides by pulling on the water that is closest to it.

Earth and Pluto are the only planets that have 1 moon. Mercury and Venus have no moons at all. All the other planets have 2 or more moons that orbit them.

The Moon is only about 238,000 miles away from Earth, which makes it closer to Earth than any other space object. It is only about $\frac{1}{4}$ the size of Earth, with a diameter of about 2,160 miles. What is the Moon's radius? You can divide its diameter by 2 to find out.

```
        1,080
    2) 2,160
      - 2
        0 1
      - 0 0
          16
        - 16
          00
```

The Moon's radius is about 1,080 miles.

Moon

The Red Planet

Mars is the fourth planet from the Sun, with an average distance from the Sun of about 141,600,000 miles. It takes Mars about 1 year and $10\frac{1}{2}$ months to complete 1 orbit around the Sun.

Mars is the second closest planet to Earth. While Venus is often called Earth's "twin," the surface of Mars is more like Earth's surface than any other planet. Almost all of Mars is covered by reddish-brown rocks, sand, and dust. Its surface is very dry and resembles Earth's deserts. In fact, scientists believe that much of Mars's surface contains a **mineral** that is also found in deserts on Earth! Mars also has deep canyons and giant volcanoes. Its highest volcano is about 3 times as high as Earth's tallest mountain, Mount Everest.

The ancient Romans named Mars after their god of war, since the planet's reddish color reminded them of the color of blood.

Scientists believe Mars is the only planet other than Earth that may have once supported life. However, Mars's surface temperature is much lower than Earth's and doesn't usually rise above 32°F, though temperatures of around 60°F have been recorded. It can get as cold as −230°F, which makes it much too cold to support the kinds of plants and animals that live on Earth.

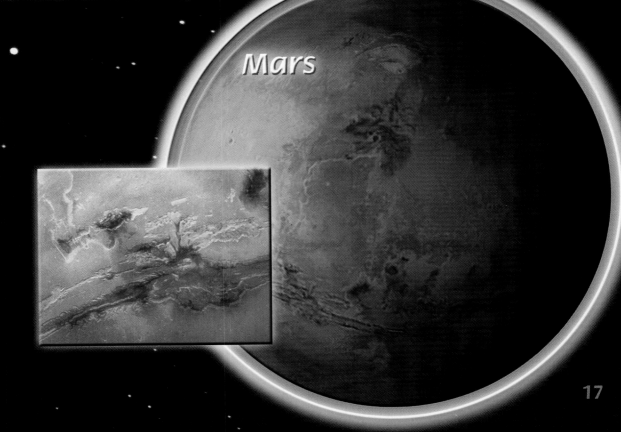

Mars

$$\begin{array}{r} 2{,}111.5 \\ 2\overline{)4{,}223.0} \\ \underline{-4}\phantom{{,}223.0} \\ 0\,2 \\ \underline{-2} \\ 0\,2 \\ \underline{-2} \\ 0\,3 \\ \underline{-2} \\ 1\,0 \\ \underline{-1\,0} \\ 0 \end{array}$$

The radius of Mars is 2,111.5 miles.

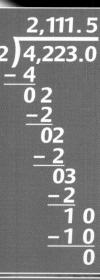

Deimos

Phobos

Both of Mars's moons are very small. In fact, a person running quickly could cover the distance of Phobos's diameter in just over 2 hours and the distance of Deimos's diameter in just over 1 hour!

Mars is the third smallest planet in the solar system—only Mercury and Pluto are smaller. The diameter of Mars is 4,223 miles, which is just slightly more than $\frac{1}{2}$ of Earth's diameter. What is the radius of Mars? We can divide its diameter by 2 to find the answer.

Mars has 2 moons. The larger moon is called Phobos (FOH-bohs). Phobos's diameter is 17 miles. The smaller moon is called Deimos (DAY-mohs). Its radius is 4.5 miles. What is its diameter? We can use either addition or multiplication to find the answer.

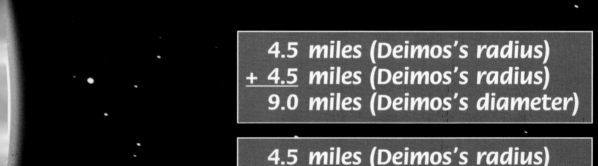

```
  4.5 miles (Deimos's radius)
+ 4.5 miles (Deimos's radius)
  9.0 miles (Deimos's diameter)
```

```
  4.5 miles (Deimos's radius)
x   2
  9.0 miles (Deimos's diameter)
```

Giant Planets

Jupiter is the fifth planet from the Sun and is made up of gas and liquid. Its average distance from the Sun is about 483,600,000 miles, which is more than 5 times the distance between Earth and the Sun. It takes Jupiter about 12 Earth years to complete its orbit around the Sun.

Jupiter is the largest planet in our solar system, with a radius of 44,423 miles. What is Jupiter's diameter? We can use either addition or multiplication to find the answer.

Jupiter has a diameter of 88,846 miles. That is more than 11 times as large as Earth's diameter and is about $\frac{1}{10}$ as large as the diameter of the Sun itself!

Jupiter

From Earth, Jupiter shines more brightly in the night sky than most stars and is usually the second brightest planet after Venus. Scientists have discovered dozens of moons orbiting Jupiter, and more are being discovered all the time. Some scientists think Jupiter may have more than 100 moons! The moons vary in size, ranging from a diameter of about 1 mile to a diameter of 3,270 miles.

$$44,423 \text{ miles (Jupiter's radius)}$$
$$\underline{44,423} \text{ miles (Jupiter's radius)}$$
$$88,846 \text{ miles (Jupiter's diameter)}$$

$$44,423 \text{ miles (Jupiter's radius)}$$
$$\underline{2}$$
$$88,846 \text{ miles (Jupiter's diameter)}$$

Ganymede

piter's largest known moon is called Ganymede.
anymede is larger than both Mercury and Pluto!

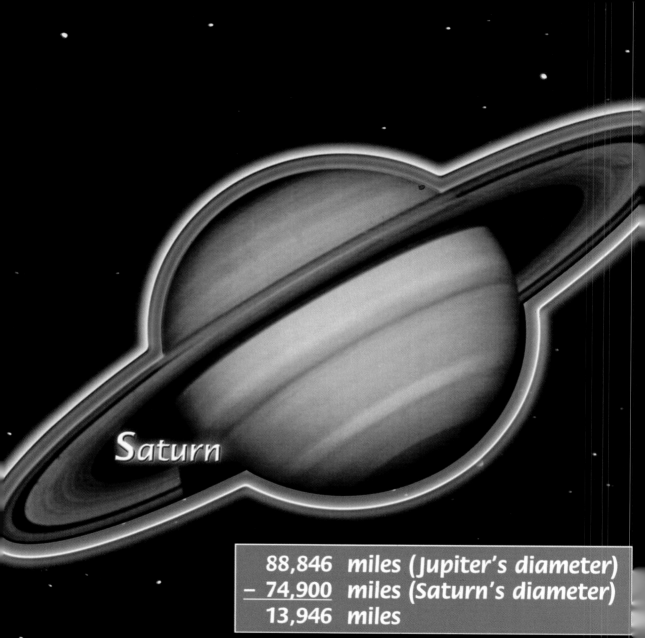

Saturn

88,846 miles (Jupiter's diameter)
− 74,900 miles (Saturn's diameter)
13,946 miles

Jupiter's diameter is 13,946 miles larger than Saturn's diameter.

Saturn is the sixth planet from the Sun. It has an average distance of 888,200,000 miles from the Sun and takes about $29\frac{1}{2}$ Earth years to complete its orbit. Many scientists think that Saturn is a huge ball of gas without a solid surface. Saturn's hot inner core, however, is thought to be made of iron and rock.

Saturn is one of the most interesting looking planets in the solar system. It has 7 large, flat rings around its **equator**. These rings are made up of thousands of smaller rings. The rings are actually billions of pieces of ice that orbit the planet. They range from tiny pieces the size of dust to large chunks with diameters of more than 10 feet!

Saturn is the second largest planet in the solar system after Jupiter. Its diameter is about 74,900 miles. How much larger is Jupiter's diameter than Saturn's diameter? We can subtract Saturn's diameter from Jupiter's diameter from page 21 to find the answer.

Saturn has 30 known moons, and some scientists think that there may be more. Titan—the largest of Saturn's moons—has a diameter of 3,200 miles. Some of Saturn's moons have a diameter of only about 2 miles.

Uranus

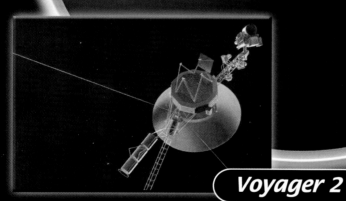

Voyager 2

On August 20, 1977, *Voyager 2* was launched from Cape Canaveral, Florida. Since then, it has traveled over 6.5 billion miles, and has traveled outside of our solar system!

```
          15,881.5
   2 ) 31,763.0
     -  2
        11
     - 10
         1 7
     - 16
          16
       -  16
           03
        -  2
            1 0
         -  1 0
              0
```

Uranus's radius is 15,881.5 miles.

The seventh planet from the Sun is Uranus. Uranus's average distance from the Sun is about 1,786,400,000 miles. It takes the planet over 84 Earth years to complete 1 orbit around the Sun.

Uranus was discovered in 1781 by a British **astronomer** named William Herschel. In 1986, a spacecraft named *Voyager 2* passed about 50,000 miles above Uranus's cloud cover. This flight taught scientists more about Uranus than they had ever known before. Uranus is made up of gas and liquid, and is covered with bluish-green clouds. Many scientists think the planet may have a rocky inner core that could be as large as Earth!

Uranus is the third largest planet in the solar system, with a diameter of 31,763 miles. That's more than 4 times as large as Earth's diameter. How much larger is Uranus's radius than Earth's diameter? Look at the problems on page 24 and this page to find the answer.

$$\begin{array}{r} 15{,}881.5 \text{ miles (Uranus's radius)} \\ -\ 7{,}926.0 \text{ miles (Earth's diameter)} \\ \hline 7{,}955.5 \text{ miles} \end{array}$$

Uranus's radius is 7,955.5 miles larger than Earth's diameter.

The Outer Planets

The two planets furthest from the Sun are Neptune and Pluto. Neither of these planets can be seen without a telescope. Neptune is the eighth planet from the Sun. Its average distance from the Sun is about 2,798,800,000 miles. That is more than 30 times greater than the distance from Earth to the Sun. It takes Neptune about 165 Earth years to orbit the Sun once.

Neptune has a radius of 15,250 miles. By doubling this, we can find Neptune's diameter.

```
  15,250 miles (Neptune's radius)
+ 15,250 miles (Neptune's radius)
  30,500 miles (Neptune's diameter)
```

```
  15,250 miles (Neptune's radius)
X      2
  30,500 miles (Neptune's diameter)
```

Neptune's diameter is 30,500 miles.

Scientists have discovered 11 moons that orbit Neptune, but only 2 of these moons can be seen from Earth through a telescope. *Voyager 2* discovered the other 9 moons in 1989. Neptune's largest moon is called Triton. Triton's surface temperature is 390°F below zero, which is the coldest recorded temperature in our solar system.

Neptune's largest moon, Triton, has a diameter of 1,680 miles. It has active volcanoes that shoot ice crystals several miles above its surface.

Little is known about Pluto because it is so far away. Pluto is an average distance of 3,666,200,000 miles from the Sun and takes about 248 Earth years to complete 1 orbit. Although Pluto is usually the furthest planet from the Sun, part of its very long, narrow orbit brings it closer to the Sun than Neptune. About every 248 years, Pluto crosses inside Neptune's orbit, where it stays for about 20 years.

Pluto is the smallest planet in our solar system. Scientists think that Pluto's diameter is only about 1,430 miles, which makes it only about $\frac{2}{3}$ as large as our Moon. Pluto's only known moon, called Charon, was discovered in 1978. Charon has a diameter of 740 miles. What is the difference between Charon's diameter and Pluto's radius? To find out, let's first figure out Pluto's radius by dividing its diameter by 2.

$$
\begin{array}{r}
715 \\
2\overline{)1{,}430} \\
-14 \\
\hline
03 \\
-2 \\
\hline
10 \\
-10 \\
\hline
0
\end{array}
$$

Pluto's radius is 715 miles.

Hubble Space Telescope

Now subtract this amount from Charon's diameter.

740	miles (Charon's diameter)
− 715	miles (Pluto's radius)
25	miles

Charon's diameter is 25 miles larger than Pluto's radius.

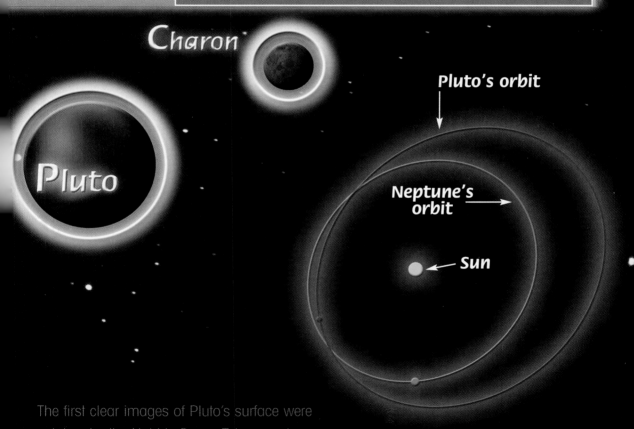

Charon

Pluto

Pluto's orbit

Neptune's orbit

Sun

The first clear images of Pluto's surface were taken by the Hubble Space Telescope in 1996. The Hubble Space Telescope orbits about 380 miles above the Earth's surface.

The Sun

The Sun has the largest diameter of any object in our solar system, measuring about 865,000 miles across! That is almost 110 times as large as Earth's diameter. Can you find the Sun's radius? You can divide its diameter by 2 to find the answer.

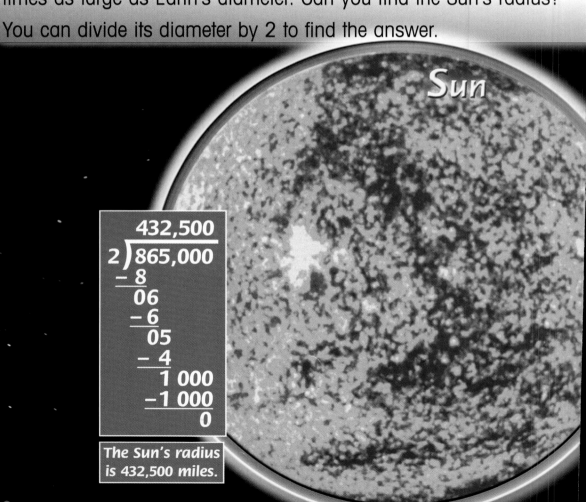

Sun

```
      432,500
  2 ) 865,000
    - 8
      06
     - 6
      05
      - 4
       1 000
      -1 000
           0
```

The Sun's radius is 432,500 miles.

Glossary

astronomer (uh-STRAH-nuh-mur) A scientist who studies the Sun, Moon, planets, stars, and other space objects.

diameter (die-AA-muh-tur) A straight line that goes from one side of a circle through the center to the other side.

equator (ee-KWAY-tur) An imaginary circle around the middle of a planet at its widest part.

gravity (GRA-vuh-tee) The force between 2 objects that attracts or pulls them toward each other.

mineral (MIH-nuh-ruhl) Something found in soil that is not an animal, plant, or other living thing.

phase (FAZE) One in a regular series of changing appearances of the Moon or a planet. These result from changes in the amount of the lighted portion of the Moon or planet visible from Earth.

radius (RAY-dee-us) Any straight line that goes from the center of a circle to its outside edge.

solar system (SOH-lur SIS-tum) The system made up of our Sun, the nine planets, moons, and other space objects.

telescope (TEH-luh-skohp) An instrument you look through that makes things that are far away look bigger and closer.

Index